# ROGER HIORNS
# @Ikon Gallery, Birmingham

# A FABRIC FULL OF HOLES
## Ruth Noack

The data stick he hands me contains more than 500 images. "They got mixed up when I copied them," he notes nonchalantly. And that is all

he says about it. If I did not know
that this is an artist who is most
eloquent — in fact, no one talks
about his work as well as he does —

I'd assume that this was some kind of mistake. As it is, the lack of functional information must mean *something*. Since we've only just met for the first time, I doubt that I can interpret this as a sign of trust. Why then does Roger Hiorns overload his author-to-be with this deluge of an

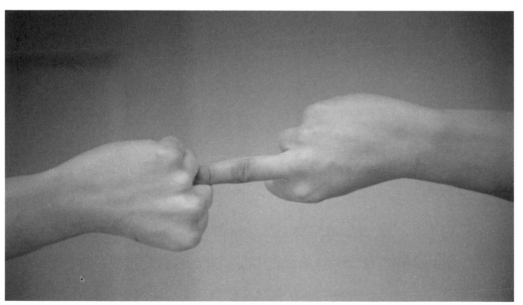

unstructured archive? What is its purpose? Some say, in chaos lies the ultimate form of control. I simply hope, for both of our sakes, that he

# knows what he is doing. All I know is that I am supposed to contribute an essay to a book of photographs.

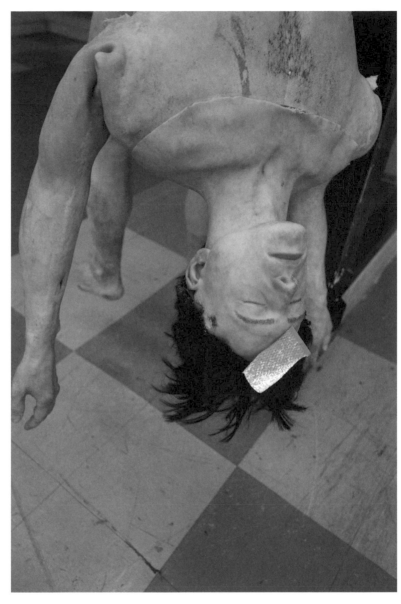

Roger Hiorns once proclaimed his
desire *not to be so stricken with
meaning*. [1] He also confessed to an
attempt, in making work, to take

himself *out of the equation*. [2]
Both sentiments are to be admired —
and sentiments they might well be,
rather than remits. For who would

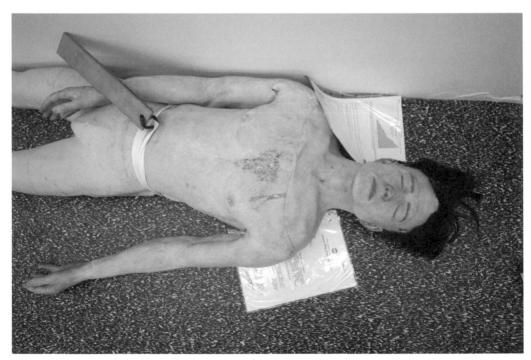

assign himself remits that cannot
be fulfilled? Nevertheless, I decide to
follow his lead, to make do with as
little meaning as possible. Yet, some

sort of exegesis will need to be written. Besides, it is hard to get rid of the author in the text.

"But what would the theorist be looking for if she wanted to find what gives a particular group of films their libidinal coherence?

# She would be searching not just for the author 'inside' the text, but for the text 'inside' the author." [3] (Kaja Silverman)

017.DE HALLEN-ROGER HIORNS 2012-PH.GJ.van ROOIJ.tif

Libidinal coherence is a concept that might actually suffice as a tool for dealing with Hiorns' group of photographs. Unity of a sort is found by its assembly on the data stick, as well as by projecting its future collation in the book. However, we are dealing with a number of quite

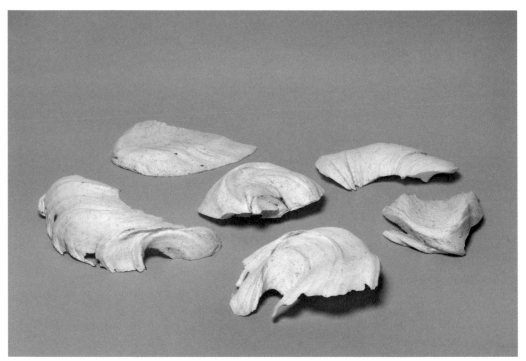

divergent sets of images: photos of
differing subjects and styles, taken
by the artist; images of art work in
situ or representing objects in isola-

tion; miscellanea collected from a
variety of sources ranging from
mainstream media to loose leaflets
to scientific tomes. Furthermore,

the number of assorted images seems
rather arbitrary; this group could
easily expand or shrink in size without losing its character. Which means

that its border cannot be used as
a marker. Here, conventional production of coherence, based on the
beginning and end of a narrative

92b9c2be8f0a05f0d737a1b37ac5d44.jpg

or supported by dichotomous meaning making (i.e. the act of defining
a core identity by excluding something as other) are suspended. We

are missing a clear definition. All
we have is an approximation, materialised in around 500 pictures.

All we have is an approximation of a corpus. And the idea that this corpus might be held together by an internal energy or desire, somehow connected to what Kaja Silverman calls *the text in the author*. Why is this relevant? Lets first address the aspect of approximation. It is a

rather precise term, describing a
thing that is similar to something
but not exactly the same, or a
movement towards something that

is never complete. I think of it as approaching something with one eye closed and one eye open or drawing by instinct rather than measure.

cathedral 1.tif

As an aesthetic practice, this indicates a renunciation of mastery.
(Or, possibly, a more subtle, refined
form of mastery?)

Yet, the gesture remains. A corpus is created, albeit one with fluid borders. As far as it exudes a whiff of esotericism, hinting at a disaffection with

domesticviolence.tif

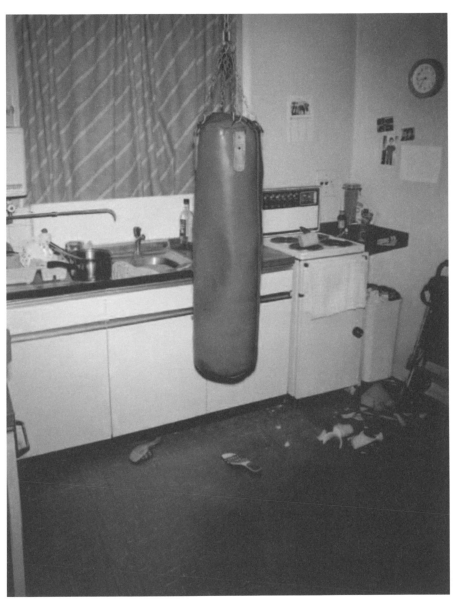

the discursive rationality displayed
in contemporary artistic practice
shaped by Cultural Studies and
Critical Theory, it can be likened to

the tradition of the cabinet of curiosities. Those private collections unified wondrous objects of fine arts as well as artefacts, biological speci-

Every week 2 women die
due to domestic violence.
Don't let your friend be 1 of them.

If you know your friend's being hit, it's time to put a stop to her abuse, before the abuser puts a stop to her. Help her take the first step; call the National Domestic Violence Helpline for support.

**ENOUGH**
**0808 2000 247**

Helpline run by Refuge and Women's Aid

mens and geological finds from all
over the planet into one display,
suggesting an organisational whole
without belying the fact that the

individual objects were chosen
almost by chance and only had an
imaginary relation to the world
at large. Thus this universe with-

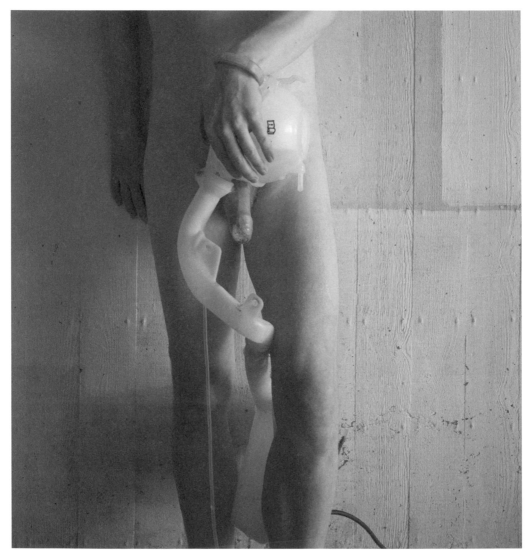

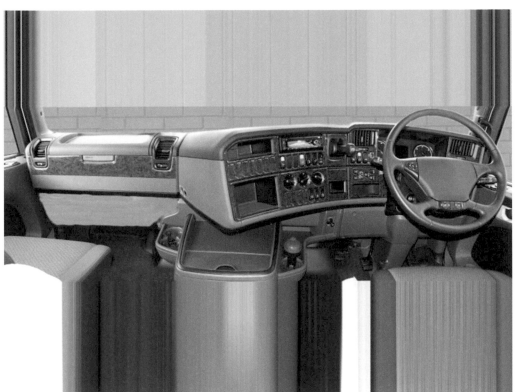

in a universe would necessarily
remain an incomplete representation
of said world.

# Both, the corpus of photographs and the cabinet of curiosities share a disdain for taxonomy, but the latter carries with it the double burden of

privileged ownership and colonialism.
Let's think outside the box, let's
think of the cabinet of curiosities
exemplifying a world through the

eyes of someone who has read Guy Debord's *The Society of the Spectacle* from 1967. Then we might use Richard Hamiton's *Just what is it that

makes today's homes so different,
so appealing?* [1956] or Martha Rosler's
*Bringing the War Home: House
Beautiful* [1967–72] v to drive a wedge

# between the anthropological value of such a collection of artefacts and the purposeful naiveté of this pre- cursor of the European museum. As

Ah! lovely 😊 memories of Prosper de Mulder, William Forrest and Robbie Dwyer loads for Grannox 😊

This image is the reason Easysheet were invented 😊

Thanks for all that! just to add that i am a vegan cc

**Re: old companys from stoke -on trent**
□by **curnock** » Fri Oct 01, 2010 8:13 pm
my first job on leaving school was for coleshill by products in cannock,on the fresh fat cookers !!!!.mmmmmmmm

**Re: old companys from stoke -on trent**
□by **Cockney Pete3** » Mon Oct 04, 2010 3:24 pm
Anyone remember Critchlows? ran canary yellow ERFs in the 80s????

**Re: old companys from stoke -on trent**
□by **Trev_H** » Mon Oct 04, 2010 5:45 pm

> **"Cockney Pete3 wrote:**
> Anyone remember Critchlows? ran canary yellow ERFs in the 80s????

Hi Pete,
Yeh I remember them, I think their trucks were also maroon colour at one time, I remember loading with them at John Thompsons (later Rockwell) in W-ton. The firm I worked for Thomas Ingles hauled trailer beam axles and Foden axle casings, Critchlows took the Albion axle casings to Scotstoun. One of their big j's with a 180 gardner had a turbo fitted to it as an experiment, after a trip to Scotland I asked the driver (lenny?) what it went like? His reply had me in stitches he said it was like any other 180 gardner bloody gutless, the only other difference was that it whistled. I think they may have done a lot of work for Shelton steelworks.

Roger Hiorns @Ikon Gallery

Debord teaches us, with modernity, the commodity has taken on the role of colonising all social life, supporting a capitalist structure of violence

which does not impact upon everyone in the same manner. Fast forward, and biopolitics need to be
figured in here, but let's take this
slowly, step by step.

age 76

age 49

age 75

age 49

'Over 40's to get dementia testing' millions exposed to Mad Cow Disease 1980's & 90's, symptoms include: anxiety, depression, memory loss, confusion, balance & coordination, stumbling, falls & difficulty walking, slurred speech, visual deteriaration, evetual blindness.

justice4andy.com
justiceforandy.com
christinelord@justiceandy

When Hiorns explains that he would like to exhibit his photographs in such a way that they present "a low value status to the viewer, perhaps in a manner similar to a universal marketing display ..." [4] he is acknowledging Debord's contribution to the way we read the world today, while,

at the same time, disavowing the
cabinet of curiosities, or rather, one
of its present forms: the private collection of contemporary art (which

# depends precisely on the value of the art work as commodity].

Brain Heart Infusion
Code - Powder CM225

FORMULA

| | | |
|---|---|---|
| Calf brain infusion solids | gram per litre | 12.5 |
| Beef heart infusion solids | | 5.0 |
| Proteose Peptone | | 10.0 |
| Dextrose | | 2.0 |
| Sodium chloride | | 5.0 |
| Disodium phosphate | | 2.5 |

pH 7.4 $\pm$ 0.2

DIRECTIONS

Powder:  Add 37 g to 1 litre of distilled water. Mix well and
distribute into final containers. Sterilize by autoclaving at
121°C for 15 minutes.

### 3.1.3 **Miscellaneous products containing Bovine Pancreas**

3.1.3.1 Zonulysin (Chymotrypsin) - Henleys Laboratories

    - sourced from Canada.

3.1.3.2 Streptokinase (Hoechst) - culture medium, containing bovine muscle and pancreas are used in process

    - all sourced from Germany.

3.1.3.3 Elase - Fibrinogen + Desoxyribonuclease (Parke-Davis)

    - bovine pancreas sourced from Canada and S Africa.

### 3.2 **Vaccines using Bovine Products in process**

3.2.1 Cyanamid - DTP vaccine (CTC) (acellular pertussis) - Beefheart from USA

3.2.2 Immuno - tick-born encephalitis vaccine - USA source (named patient use, unlicensed)

3.2.3 Merieux - Meningitis Vaccine - Muller Hinton medium containing beef

    - source not known

Tuberculin - Imotest - Beef heart and peptone

Typhoid - Vi - source not known

3.2.4 PHLS - Anthrax Vaccine - Peptone, casein and meat of bovine origin

    - source "probably N.America"

Adult diphtheria vaccine - bovine muscle - source Swizterland

Hiorns also sidesteps another trope, that of the creator of an idiosyncratic artistic universe, exemplified by figures like Joseph Beuys or Martin

# Kippenberger. While I don't deny that the agents of this trope deal with material that is as much *in and of the world* as that presented

by Hiorns, its unifying force remains the masculine artist-subject, the central author in the text. More often than not, humanist universalism is

carried forth in this kind of work
even in those instances where the
artist eagerly posits himself against
modernity, with its incorporative

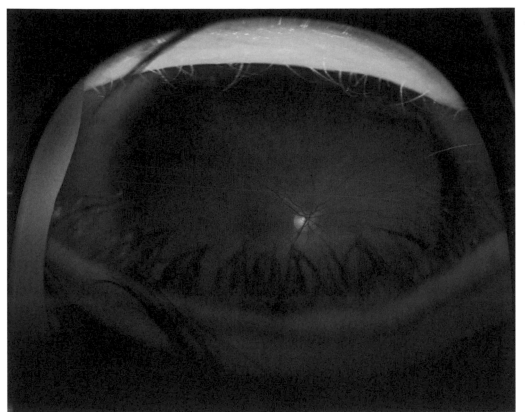

logic and master narrative. I believe
that Hiorns strives to break with
this kind of artist-subjectivity and
that he is much more interested to

think about the text in the author than the author in the text. But I would go even a step further with this artist who is struggling to take

nissel 10.jpg

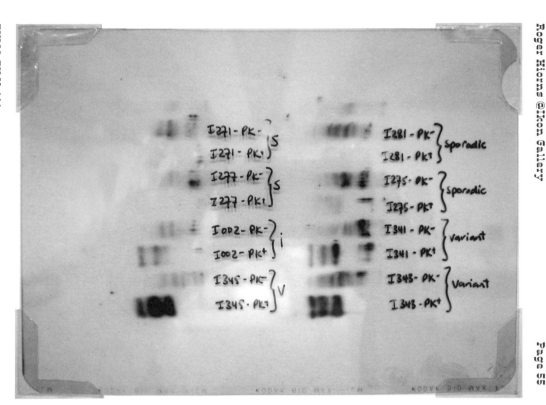

himself out of the equation, and claim
that while *the text in the author*
might be a personal motive to start
thinking with visual means, Hiorns

# is even more concerned with the *text within the text*.

ome SS211028 Streetmap Google EX23 0JE (472m) 50 47 51.540 N 4 32 20.694 W 0m 1m 1m 10000m

*lap © Ordnance Survey*

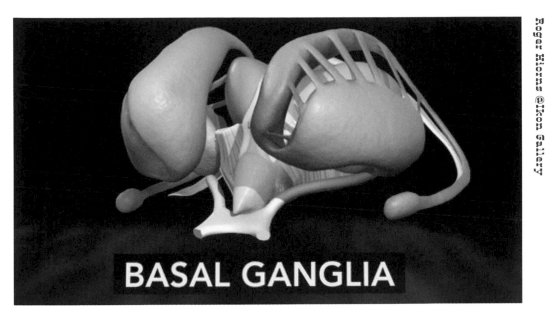

BASAL GANGLIA

What is the *text within the text*?
Before I try to understand and an-
swer this, let's backtrack. Roger
Hiorns uses different tools to punch

holes into the fabric that holds the work of art in its fetishised place. Where the figure of the artist-subject serves as parameter for the

(e)valuation of the artistic output,
he plays at self-effacement. Where
conventionalised systems of knowledge take on the function of valori-

sation, he insists on countering
meaning-production. Where identity
and taxonomy threaten the ability
of a work of art to offer itself to its

viewers as an object of aesthetic
experience, he undermines them by
means of overload and approximation.
In his show on the variant Creutz-

feldt-Jakob disease (vCJD), for example, he deliberately engulfs his
viewers in a flood of extremely complex material that *requires a huge

amount of unraveling, close reading
and cross-examination*. He explains,
"It has been important to propose
'too much', to create a short-circuit of

# information, to simply allow the viewer to make their own path through the subject." [5]

**April 2001**

At this time, 101 cattle born after 31 July 1996 have been slaughtered under suspicion of BSE. Of those in Great Britain, one was BSE positive, 167 were BSE negative and results are pending for three. No additional case born after 31 July 1996 has occurred in Northern Ireland.

**2001**

The Department for Environment, Food & Rural Affairs (DEFRA) is founded. It brings together environment, wildlife and countryside remits from the former Department of the Environment, Transport and the Regions with all the functions of the former MAFF (the Ministry of Agriculture, Fisheries and Food).

**May 2001**

The American Red Cross, which collects around half of the US blood supply, tightens its restrictions on blood donations from people who have spent time in Europe. It stops taking blood from individuals who have spent as little as three months in Britain, or six months anywhere in Europe, at any time from 1980.

**2001**

Epidemiological studies to date have failed to demonstrate that scrapie can be transferred to humans; however, there is evidence suggesting that scrapie was transmitted to cattle, thereby initiating the European mad cow epidemic.

**19 August 2001**

The Foot and Mouth epidemic reaches the six-month mark with 3,750,222 animals slaughtered, and 2,000 confirmed cases. The tourist trade says local businesses have lost an estimated £250m.

**5 March 2001**

The Department of Health Reports that the total number of definite and probable cases of vCJD so far is 95. This figure includes 9 probable deaths from vCJD where neuropathological confirmation will never be possible.

Changes in
behaviour,
activity and
mental status

Animal Health and Plant Agency
*Clinical Signs of Bovine Spongiform
Encephalopathy in Cattle* 2013
DVD. Duration 35 mins
Courtesy Animal Health and Plant Agency

But then again, Roger Hiorns works at evading aestheticised readings of his art by intervening into the discourse around his practice with careful debasement of all that might be appreciated by a viewer in a purely formal way. A further strategy against aestheticisation is to tamper

with the form of his work. For instance, one must wonder why an
artist who has generated seductive
crystal growths and covers canvas

with brain matter would be so hard
set on *acting against the surface*? [6]
This is not just something Hiorns
only proclaims in theory. By photo-

graphing his art objects and exhibitions (or having them photographed)
he is subtracting from them their
haptic materiality, their surface aes-

# thetic. And while even snapshots of photos of inferior quality can be fetishised, their merging with the range of other photos included in

the corpus, works against their
status as singular objects of special
value. I believe that Hiorns does this
exactly because he is aware of what

the philosopher Peter Osborne calls "the critical necessity of an anti-aestheticist use of aesthetic materials" within post-conceptual art. [7]

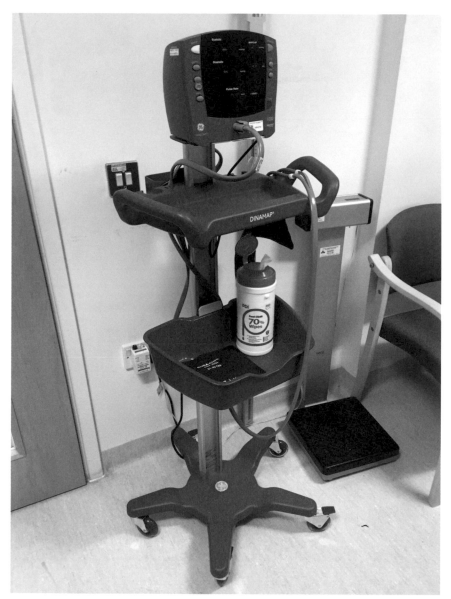

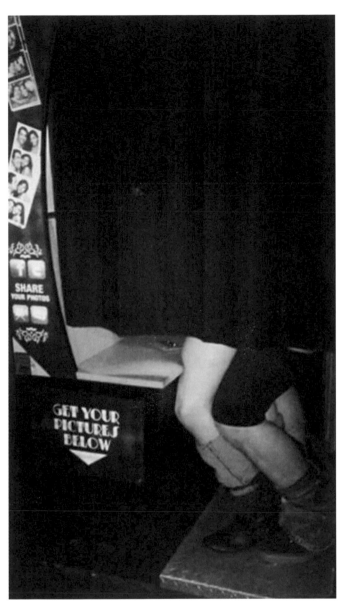

And thus we return to the text within the text. By defining Roger Hiorns corpus of photographs as a text, I mean no more than to propose

to 'read' the images. After all, I had
promised some kind of exegesis at
the outset of my musings. Reading
images is not just something for art

NOT RACIST
NOT VIOLENT
NO LONGER SI

30    ★ 14    •••

●●●●○ O2-UK 🛜 09:21 ✳ 100% ▭

theguardian.com ↻

historians, curators or art critics
to do in their spare time, it is also a
practice of everyday life. But most
importantly, it is a way to start un-

derstanding how our ways of seeing the world are influenced by the visual formations around us. By reading images, we are not just honing our

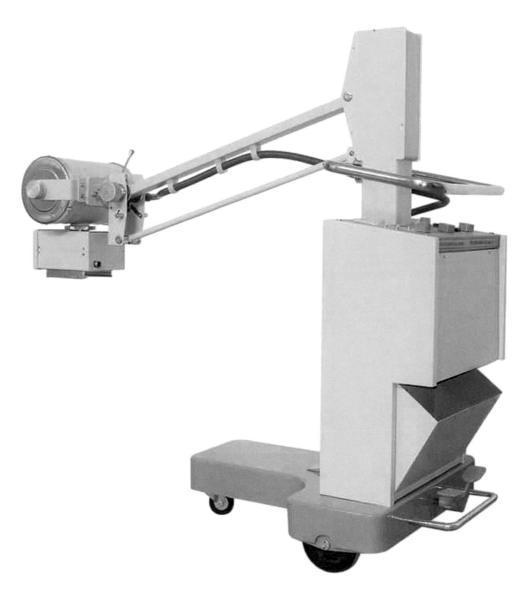

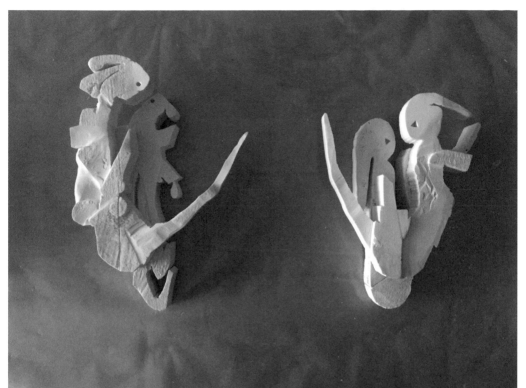

visual skills, but actively engaging
in piecing together a segment of the
order which determines our visuality
in its historically specific formation.

# It is within this visual order that subjects appear and move — and potentially move to reaffirm or change the framework itself. This is the

stuff of any beginner's guide to
Michel Foucault and Jacques Lacan,
though I am being a little fuzzy here,
with my terminology referring in an

approximate way to both, Foucault's
*dispositif* and Lacan's *screen*.
Kaja Silverman would maintain, with
Lacan, that the framework I am talk-

ing about cannot be individually
changed, because it is regulated by
the gaze, an entity entirely out of
reach by individual subjectivity.

# But Silverman also claims, this is back in the 1990s, that artistic production may, from time to time, manage to rework the screen ... [8]

What then, is *the text within* the corpus of photographs? It was already intimated that libido would be involved. One should probably speak

about desire, but I will be crass and
call it sex. However, there is more
*text within* to be had: What else
determines how we see, i.e. visualise

things? Possibly, the empirical,
spatial and object-based structures
within our contemporary habitat?
*The text within* pertains to the

way we perform in daily life, or to the way our experiences and tastes are structured by what we encounter from childhood on. *The text within*

concerns the way in which we perceive our bodies within an environment. Finally, *the text within*
deals with the way our subjectivity

coalesces with normative social
signifiers such as class-race-gender
— or fails to do so.

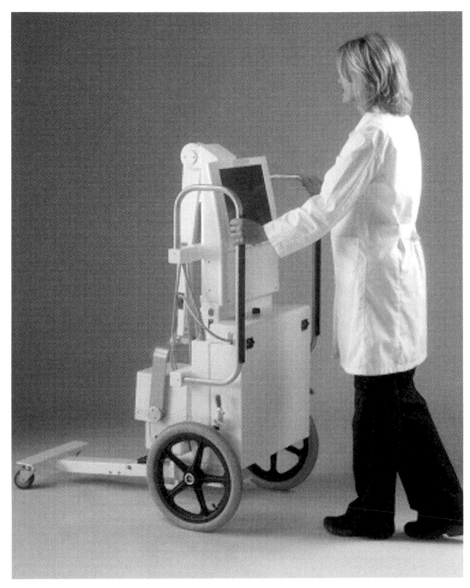

As part of \*this text\* that is actually \*within\* Roger Hiorns visual production, I would want to emphasise biopolitics, the social and political

power over life, as one of its most
notable aspects. Due to the data-
'mishap' I have no way of knowing
whether any of the images and

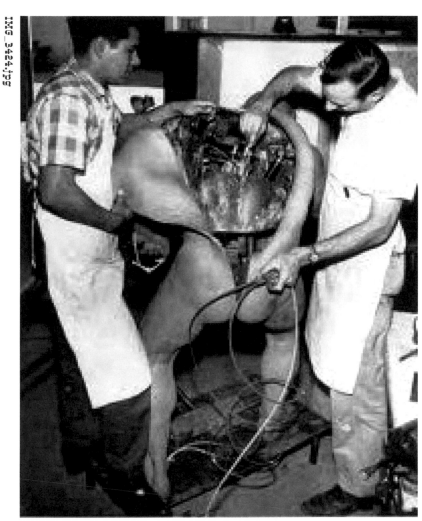

documents from Hiorns' vCJD show
will end up in his book of photographs. That show concerned itself
with the ongoing health crisis that

ended up binding together the failure of the British government with
the public's loss of faith in any
governance at all, its reverberations

felt until today. As Hiorns states:
"The threat that the disease poses
to national and global health is
still considerable ... Perhaps as a

consequence of our increasingly
predatory capitalist environment,
such potential health risks are increasingly seen as unavoidable —

merely part of the system that we exist within, a population caught in the binding chain of systemic violence." [9] Roger Hiorns' concern with biopolitics, which leads him to engage in the social and aesthetical fabric of present-day existence, puncturing the Lacanian screen here and

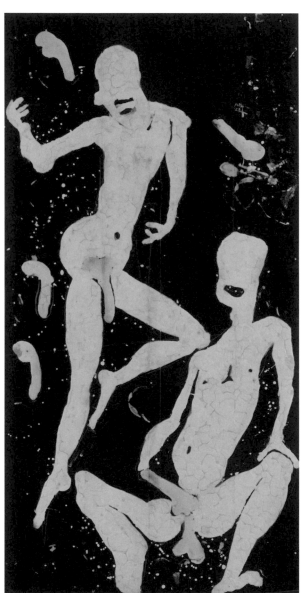

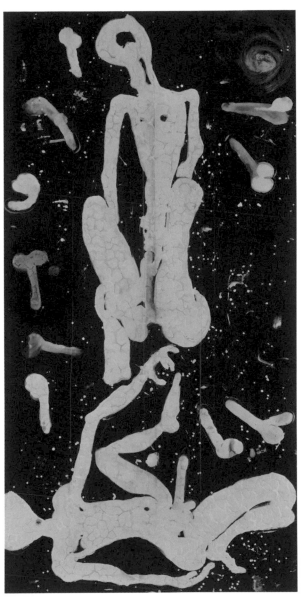

there, until it reveals itself to us in-deed as a fabric full of holes, is seri-ous. And it needs to be taken seriously.

# With the fervour of that last statement as a guide, I will attempt to approximate some of the libidinal energy that circulates more or less

FOR YOUR SAFETY YOU MUST WEAR SUITABLE BARRIER CLOTHING AND MASKS.

**perceptibly through the corpus, as
well as through my text, with a few
loose groupings of some of the photographs. My choices are being steered**

# by those photographs which have most successfully cathected me. The titles are entirely mine.

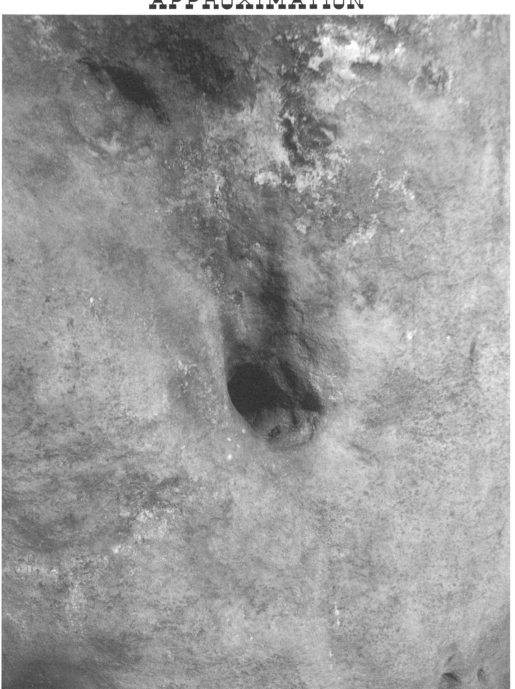

# OEDIPUS

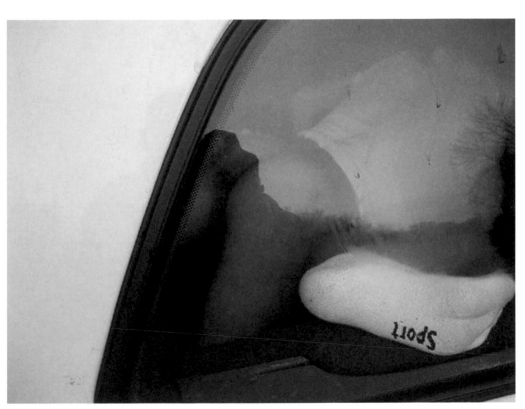

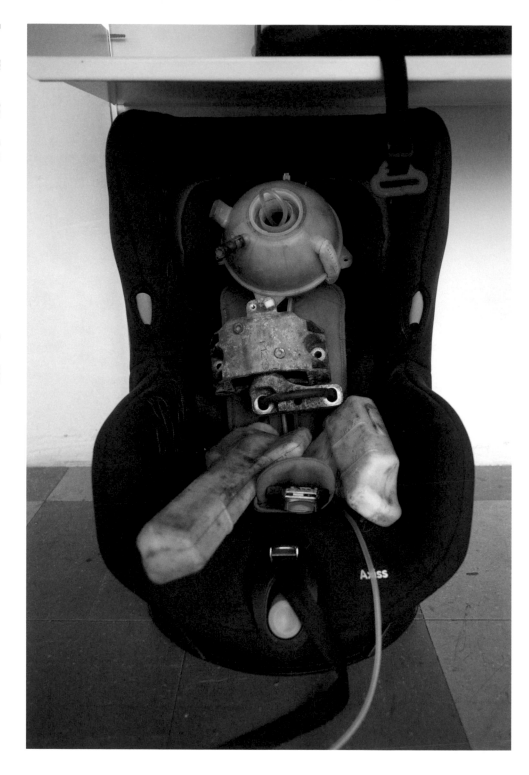

# THE CRADLE OF CIVILISATION

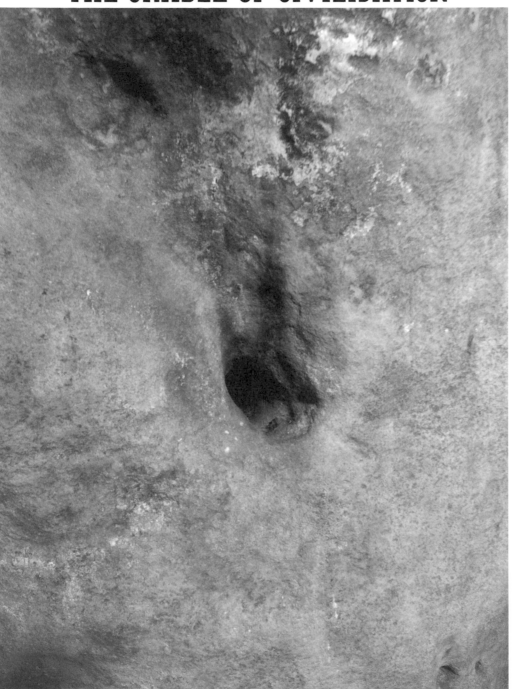

# CIVILISATION UNDONE

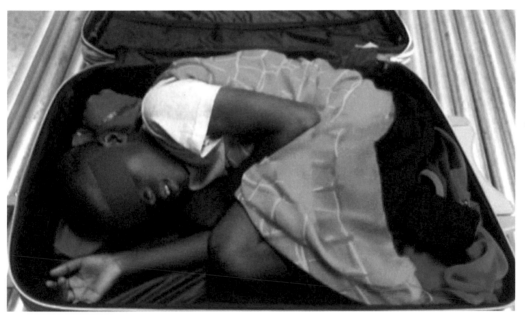

# ANTHROPOLOGY

# OBJECT PETIT A

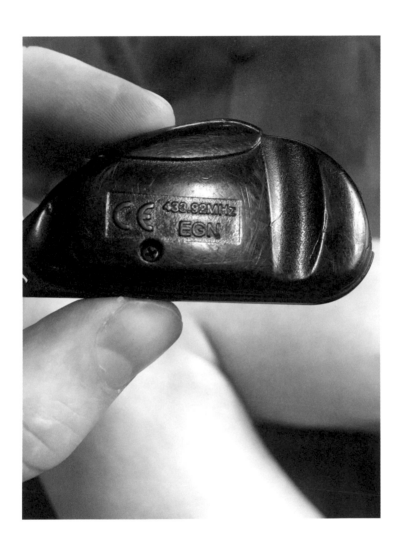

# TWO SIDES OF A COIN – CAPITALISM

4

# ANOTHER TWO SIDES OF A COIN – BIOPOLITICS

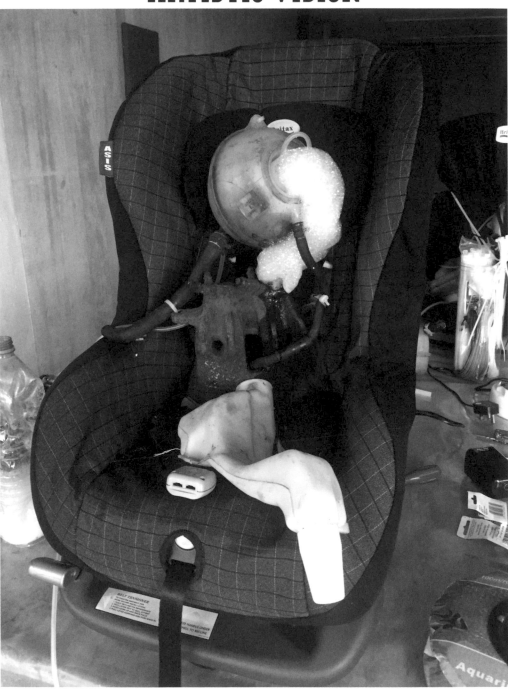

# MESSES IN THE AFTERNOON

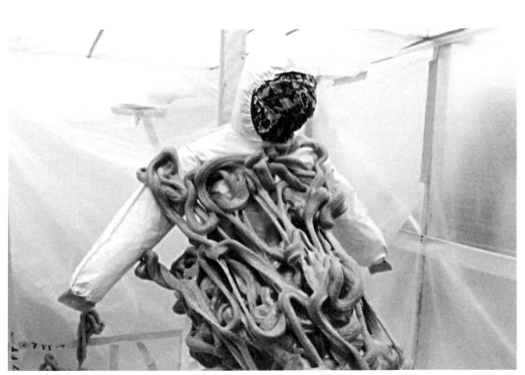

# WALTER BENJAMIN'S CRYSTAL

# FOOTNOTES

[1]      'The Impregnation of an Object. Roger Hiorns in Conversation with James Lingwood', *Seizure*, Artangel, London 2008, p.71.

[2]      Ibid, p.70.

[3]      Kaja Silverman, *The Acoustic Mirror. The Female Voice in Psychoanalysis and Cinema*, Indiana University Press, Bloomington and Indianapolis 1988, p.216.

[4]      Felicity Lunn, 'Interview with Roger Hiorns', *Roger Hiorns*, Verlag für modern Kunst, Vienna 2015, p.39.

[5]      Roger Hiorns, 'The population is now waking up from its well-managed slumber because of these successive public abuses', *History is Now: 7 Artists Take on Britain*, Hayward Publishing, London 2015, p.130.

[6]      Quoted in Felicity Lunn, op. cit., p.33.

[7]      Peter Osborne, *Anywhere or Not at All: Philosophy of Contemporary Art*, Verso, London and New York 2013, p.48.

[8]      Kaja Silverman, *The Threshold of the Visible World*, Routledge, London and New York, 1996.

[9]      Roger Hiorns, op. cit., p.130.

# APPENDIX

Ruth Noack

## A Fabric Full of Holes

The data stick he hands me contains more than 500 images. "They got mixed up when I copied them," he notes nonchalantly. And that is all he says about it. If I did not know that this is an artist who is most eloquent – in fact, no one talks about his work as well as he does – I'd assume that this was some kind of mistake. As it is, the lack of functional information must mean *something*. Since we've only just met for the first time, I doubt that I can interpret this as a sign of trust. Why then does Roger Hiorns overload his author-to-be with this deluge of an unstructured archive? What is its purpose? Some say, in chaos lies the ultimate form of control. I simply hope, for both of our sakes, that he knows what he is doing. All I know is that I am supposed to contribute an essay to a book of photographs.

Roger Hiorns once proclaimed his desire *not to be so stricken with meaning.* [1] He also confessed to an attempt, in making work, to *take himself out of the equation.* [2] Both sentiments are to be admired – and sentiments they might well be, rather than remits. For who would assign himself remits that cannot be fulfilled? Nevertheless, I decide to follow his lead, to make do with as little meaning as possible. Yet, some sort of exegesis will need to be written. Besides, it is hard to get rid of the author in the text.

> But what would the theorist be looking for if she wanted to find what gives a particular group of films their libidinal coherence? She would be searching not just for the author "inside" the text, but for the text "inside" the author. [3] (Kaja Silverman)

Libidinal coherence is a concept that might actually suffice as a tool for dealing with Hiorns' group of photographs. Unity of a sort is found by its assembly on the data stick, as well as by projecting its future collation in the book. However, we are dealing with a number of quite divergent sets of images: photos of differing subjects and styles, taken by the artist; images of art work in situ or representing objects in isolation; miscellanea collected from a variety of sources ranging from mainstream media to loose leaflets to scientific tomes. Furthermore, the number of assorted images seems rather arbitrary; this group could easily expand or shrink in size without losing its character. Which means that its border cannot be used as a marker. Here, conventional production of coherence, based on the beginning and end of a narrative or supported by dichotomous meaning making (i.e. the act of defining a core identity by excluding something as other) are suspended. We are missing a clear definition. All we have is an approximation, materialised in around 500 pictures.

All we have is an approximation of a corpus. And the idea that this corpus might be held together by an internal energy or desire, somehow connected to what Kaja Silverman calls *the text in the author*. Why is this relevant? Lets first address the aspect of approximation. It is a rather precise term, describing a thing that is similar to something but not exactly the same, or a movement towards something that is never complete. I think of it as approaching something with one eye closed and one eye open or drawing by instinct rather than measure. As an aesthetic practice, this indicates a renunciation of mastery. (Or, possibly, a more subtle, refined form of mastery?)

Yet, the gesture remains. A corpus is created, albeit one with fluid borders. As far as it exudes a whiff of esotericism, hinting at a disaffection with the discursive rationality displayed in contemporary artistic practice shaped by Cultural Studies and Critical Theory, it can be likened to the tradition of the cabinet of curiosities. Those private collections unified wondrous objects of fine arts as well as artefacts, biological specimens and geological finds from all over the planet into one display, suggesting an organisational whole without belying the fact that the individual objects were chosen almost by chance and only had an imaginary relation to the world at large. Thus this universe within a universe would necessarily remain an incomplete representation of said world.

Both, the corpus of photographs and the cabinet of curiosities share a disdain for taxonomy, but the latter carries with it the double burden of privileged ownership and colonialism. Let's think outside the box, let's think of the cabinet of curiosities exemplifying a world through the eyes of someone who has read Guy Debord's *The Society of the Spectacle* from 1967. Then we might use Richard Hamilton's *Just what is it that makes today's homes so different, so appealing?* (1956) or Martha Rosler's *Bringing the War Home: House Beautiful* (1967–72) to drive a wedge between the anthropological value of such a collection of artefacts and the purposeful naiveté of this precursor of the European museum. As Debord teaches us, with modernity, the commodity has taken on the role of colonising all social life, supporting a capitalist structure of violence which does not impact upon everyone in the same manner. Fast forward, and biopolitics need to be figured in here, but let's take this slowly, step by step.

When Hiorns explains that he would like to exhibit his photographs in such a way that they present "a low value status to the viewer, perhaps in a manner similar to a universal marketing display ..." [4] he is acknowledging Debord's contribution to the way we read the world today, while, at the same time, disavowing the cabinet of curiosities, or rather, one of its present forms: the private collection of contemporary art (which depends precisely on the value of the art work as commodity).

Hiorns also sidesteps another trope, that of the creator of an idiosyncratic artistic universe, exemplified by figures like Joseph Beuys or Martin Kippenberger. While I don't deny that the agents of this trope deal with material that is as much *in and of the world* as that presented by Hiorns, its unifying force remains the masculine artist-subject, the central author in the text. More often than not, humanist universalism is carried forth in this kind of work even in those instances where the artist eagerly posits himself against modernity, with its incorporative logic and master narrative. I believe that Hiorns strives to break with this kind of artist-subjectivity and that he is much more interested to think about the text in the author than the author in the text. But I would go even a step further with this artist who is struggling to take himself out of the equation, and claim that while *the text in the author* might be a personal motive to start thinking with visual means, Hiorns is even more concerned with *the text within the text*.

What is the *text within the text*? Before I try to understand and answer this, let's backtrack. Roger Hiorns uses different tools to punch holes into the fabric that holds the work of art in its fetishised place. Where the figure of the artist-subject serves as parameter for the (e)valuation of the artistic output, he plays at self-effacement. Where conventionalised systems of knowledge take on the function of valorisation, he insists on countering meaning-production. Where identity and taxonomy threaten the ability of a work of art to offer itself to its viewers as an object of aesthetic experience, he undermines them by means of overload and approximation. In his show on the variant Creutzfeldt-Jakob disease (vCJD), for example, he deliberately engulfs his viewers in a flood of extremely complex material that *requires a huge amount of unraveling, close reading and cross-examination*. He explains, "It has been important to propose 'too much', to create a short-circuit of information, to simply allow the viewer to make their own path through the subject." (5)

But then again, Roger Hiorns works at evading aestheticised readings of his art by intervening into the discourse around his practice with careful debasement of all that might be appreciated by a viewer in a purely formal way. A further strategy against aestheticisation is to tamper with the form of his work. For instance, one must wonder why an artist who has generated seductive crystal growths and covers canvas with brain matter would be so hard set on *acting against the surface*? (6) This is not just something Hiorns only proclaims in theory. By photographing his art objects and exhibitions (or having them photographed) he is subtracting from them their haptic materiality, their surface aesthetic. And while even snapshots of photos of inferior quality can be fetishised, their merging with the range of other photos included in the corpus, works against their status as singular objects of special value. I believe that Hiorns does this exactly because he is aware of what the philosopher Peter Osborne calls "the critical necessity of an anti-aestheticist use of aesthetic materials" within post-conceptual art. [7]

And thus we return to *the text within the text*. By defining Roger Hiorns corpus of photographs as a text, I mean no more than to propose to 'read' the images. After all, I had promised some kind of exegesis at the outset of my musings. Reading images is not just something for art historians, curators or art critics to do in their spare time, it is also a practice of everyday life. But most importantly, it is a way to start understanding how our ways of seeing the world are influenced by the visual formations around us. By reading images, we are not just honing our visual skills, but actively engaging in piecing together a segment of the order which determines our visuality in its historically specific formation. It is within this visual order that subjects appear and move — and potentially move to reaffirm or change the framework itself. This is the stuff of any beginner's guide to Michel Foucault and Jacques Lacan, though I am being a little fuzzy here, with my terminology referring in an approximate way to both, Foucault's *dispositif* and Lacan's *screen*. Kaja Silverman would maintain, with Lacan, that the framework I am talking about cannot be individually changed, because it is regulated by the gaze, an entity entirely out of reach by individual subjectivity. But Silverman also claims, this is back in the 1990s, that artistic production may, from time to time, manage to rework the screen ... [8]

What then, is *the text within* the corpus of photographs? It was already intimated that libido would be involved. One should probably speak about desire, but I will be crass and call it sex. However, there is more *text within* to be had: What else determines how we see, i.e. visualise things? Possibly, the empirical, spatial and object-based structures within our contemporary habitat? The text *within* pertains to the way we perform in daily life, or to the way our experiences and tastes are structured by what we encounter from childhood on. *The text within* concerns the way in which we perceive our bodies within an environment.

Finally, *the text within* deals with the way our subjectivity coalesces with normative social signifiers such as class-race-gender – or fails to do so.

As part of *this text* that is actually *within* Roger Hiorns visual production, I would want to emphasise biopolitics, the social and political power over life, as one of its most notable aspects. Due to the data-'mishap' I have no way of knowing whether any of the images and documents from Hiorns' vCJD show will end up in his book of photographs. That show concerned itself with the on-going health crisis that ended up binding together the failure of the British government with the public's loss of faith in any governance at all, its reverberations felt until today. As Hiorns states: "The threat that the disease poses to national and global health is still considerable ... Perhaps as a consequence of our increasingly predatory capitalist environment, such potential health risks are increasingly seen as unavoidable – merely part of the system that we exist within, a population caught in the binding chain of systemic violence."[9] Roger Hiorns' concern with biopolitics, which leads him to engage in the social and aesthetical fabric of present-day existence, puncturing the Lacanian screen here and there, until it reveals itself to us indeed as a fabric full of holes, is serious. And it needs to be taken seriously.

With the fervour of that last statement as a guide, I will attempt to approximate some of the libidinal energy that circulates more or less perceptibly through the corpus, as well as through my text, with a few loose groupings of some of the photographs. My choices are being steered by those photographs which have most success-fully cathected me. The titles are entirely mine.

# Footnotes

(1)     'The Impregnation of an Object. Roger Hiorns in Conversation with James Lingwood', *Seizure*, Artangel, London 2008, p.71.

(2)     *Ibid*, p.70.

(3)     Kaja Silverman, *The Acoustic Mirror. The Female Voice in Psychoanalysis and Cinema*, Indiana University Press, Bloomington and Indianapolis 1988, p.216.

(4)     Felicity Lunn, 'Interview with Roger Hiorns', *Roger Hiorns*, Verlag für modern Kunst, Vienna 2015, p.39.

(5)     Roger Hiorns, 'The population is now waking up from its well-managed slumber because of these successive public abuses', *History is Now: 7 Artists Take on Britain*, Hayward Publishing, London 2015, p.130.

(6)     Quoted in Felicity Lunn, op. cit., p.33.

(7)     Peter Osborne, *Anywhere or Not at All: Philosophy of Contemporary Art*, Verso, London and New York 2013, p.48.

(8)     Kaja Silverman, *The Threshold of the Visible World*, Routledge, London and New York, 1996.

(9)     Roger Hiorns, op. cit., p.130.

# COLOPHON

Roger Hiorns
7 December 2016 – 5 March 2017

Curated by Jonathan Watkins
Assisted by Roma Piotrowska

Ikon Gallery
1 Oozells Square
Brindleyplace
Birmingham B1 2HS
UK

Roger Hiorns' exhibition is supported by
Corvi-Mora, London;
Annet Gelink, Amsterdam;
Luhring Augustine, New York and the Ikon Investment Fund.
Ikon is supported using public funding by Arts Council England
and Birmingham City Council.

www.ikon-gallery.org

Edited by Jonathan Watkins
Text by Ruth Noack
Designed by Studio Felix Salut
Typefaces: Pareto, Dinamo; (www.abcdinamo.com);
Landnáma, Or Type (www.ortype.is)
Printed by Ruksaldruck, Berlin

ISBN: 978-1-911155-06-5

Distributed by Cornerhouse Publications
Cornerhouse Publications, HOME,
2 Tony Wilson Place, Manchester M15 4FN, UK

T: +44 (0) 161 2123466 and +44 (0) 161 2123468
Email: publications@cornerhouse.org

artist if you nevertheless feel there has been an error or infringement of copyright.

**IKON**

Photography:
John Collinge,
    p. 55;
Greenpeace,
    61, 112;
Roger Hiorns,
    as part of the archive work *Digestive System* (1998–ongoing),
    pp. 9–11, 13–14, 19, 24–29, 32–42, 48–51, 53–54, 56–58, 60, 62–65,
    69–81, 83, 89–91, 98–111, 113–124, 126–128, 129 (with thanks to
    Conrad Atkinson), 130–136;
Marcus Leith,
    p. 8, 12, 16–17, 20, 52, 66–68, 82, 92–97;
Christine Lord,
    pp. 43–47, 125;
Chris Keenan,
    pp. 84–88;
Marcin Szymczak:
    p. 15, 30–31;
Jason Wyche:
    p. 59;
Gert Jan van Rooij,
    p. 18;
Brian Fitzsimmons,
    pp. 21–22, 23;

Photography cover:
Jason Evans,
photographed for Christie's Magazine, 2016

Roger Hiorns would like to thank:
Anastasia Hiorns
Hal Hiorns
Joseph K
Nick Skipp
Angus McCrum